YOGA

FOR BEGINNERS

MAREN SCHWICHTENBERG

MEYER
& MEYER
SPORT

Original title: Yoga für Einsteiger
© Meyer & Meyer, Aachen, 2006
Translated by Heather Ross

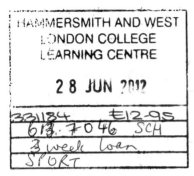
British Library Cataloguing in Publication Data
A catalogue record for this book is available from the British Library

Maren Schwichtenberg
YOGA FOR BEGINNERS
Oxford: Meyer & Meyer Sport (UK) Ltd., 2007
ISBN-10: 1-84126-195-5
ISBN-13: 978-1-84126-195-9

© 2007 by Meyer & Meyer Sport (UK) Ltd.
Aachen, Adelaide, Auckland, Budapest, Graz, Johannesburg, New York,
Olten (CH), Oxford, Singapore, Toronto
 Member of the World
Sports Publishers' Association (WSPA)
www.w-s-p-a.org

Printed and bound by: B.O.S.S Druck und Medien GmbH, Germany
ISBN-10: 1-84126-195-5
ISBN-13: 978-1-84126-195-9
E-Mail: verlag@m-m-sports.com
www.m-m-sports.com

Contents

Foreword

Yoga is now very popular in this country, and the fact that it has been growing in popularity for many years shows that it is not just a passing fad.

It is important that yoga is taught seriously and knowledgeably. This book is a competent guide to making yoga more than just a superficial form of gymnastics. Beginners can gain a comprehensive understanding of yoga and learn how to perform it properly, without overtaxing themselves. The individual asanas (poses) are presented in great detail with the aid of clear photos and descriptions. Beginners come to yoga with differing levels of physical fitness, so several variations are given for each asana. Warm-up exercises provide a gentle and methodical preparation for the yoga session to follow, so that people with all kinds of levels of flexibility and strength can practice yoga enjoyably and successfully.

The chapters on breathing, relaxation and meditation show how exertion and relaxation can be combined. In this way, even beginners can relax while performing the often difficult exercises.

This book presents the Rishikesh Series. This is a very effective sequence of yoga exercises, as taught at Yoga Vidya. Yoga Vidya is the largest Yoga training institute in Europe, with its headquarters in Horn-Bad Meinberg (Germany) and its own Yoga Teachers' Federation (BYV).

This book is an excellent manual to guide readers through the different asanas. The 10 sessions for beginners and the special training programs are also very useful.

I am delighted that Maren Schwichtenberg, a Yoga Vidya student who has gone on to become a yoga teacher trainer herself, is spreading the word of yoga in this highly professional way.

At this point, I would like to mention that even the best book is no substitute for the personal attention, instruction and correction of an experienced yoga teacher.

May learning and practicing yoga bring you enjoyment and well-being!

Sudakev Bretz
Chairman, Yoga Teachers' Federation (BYV)
www.yoga-vidya.de/en/

Introduction

This book is intended for people of all ages who want to improve their health by practicing yoga.

To be able to cope with the stresses of everyday life, you need to look after your mind and spirit, not just your body.

You don't need to develop bulky muscles or to be as flexible as an Olympic gymnast to practice yoga. This book was written for normal people who are looking for an introduction to yoga or those who already have some experience and want to improve by practicing on their own.

This book contains exercises for breathing, mobilization, strengthening, improving flexibility, relaxation, harmonizing and improving concentration.

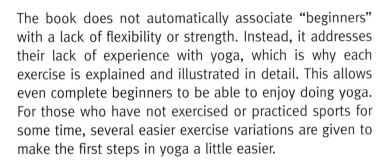

The book does not automatically associate "beginners" with a lack of flexibility or strength. Instead, it addresses their lack of experience with yoga, which is why each exercise is explained and illustrated in detail. This allows even complete beginners to be able to enjoy doing yoga. For those who have not exercised or practiced sports for some time, several easier exercise variations are given to make the first steps in yoga a little easier.

This book shows how the positive effects of doing the exercises correctly and in the right order can improve your well-being.

Experts from the field of physical fitness recommend yoga as a way of clearing the mind, strengthening the nerves and muscles and generally improving health, making it possible to live longer with a better quality of life.

Read "What is Yoga?" in the first section. If it is too late for you to use yoga for preventive purposes, and your mobility and/or load-bearing abilities are already limited.

In the chapter "Exercises Step by Step," 48 exercises are illustrated with clear and helpful photos and accompanied by thorough descriptions of how to perform them correctly and their effects.

Basic tips and fifteen example sessions are listed in the "Training Programs" chapter for you to use to build your own yoga session.

What is Yoga?

Types of Yoga

Yoga is not just an activity that relaxes or energizes; its effects go beyond just the physical, for it can bring inner contentment, feelings of happiness, insight and understanding of life, as well as other benefits.

There are many different yoga paths that lead to this state of harmony with oneself. The highest goal of a yogi is enlightenment (samadhi), in which he can know his inner self, thereby freeing himself from outside influences. One of these ways is raja yoga, the yoga of meditation. To be able to sit up straight, and concentrate in a meditation posture without moving requires some physical training, which is where hatha yoga comes in. Hatha yoga is a combination of physical poses (asanas) and breathing exercises (pranayama). Only with a healthy body and calm breathing can you manage the difficult task of meditation.

History

Yoga has been practiced for several thousand years in India. This is why the names of the exercises are all in Sanskrit, the oldest Indian language. The word "yoga" can be translated as "unity" or "harmony."

One syllable in Sanskrit is "om" [symbol] (pronounced "Ohmm"). It is also called the spoken essence of the universe. It is often said at the beginning and end of the yoga session to bring the body and mind into harmony.

Yoga Master

Swami Sivananda (1887-1963) and Swami Vishnu Devananda (1927-1993), two famous Indian yoga masters put together a Hatha Yoga teaching series in line with ancient traditions, geared toward the needs of Westerners. Swami Vishnu Devananda was one of the yoga masters who brought yoga to the West (USA, Canada, Europe).

Hatha Yoga

"Ha" means "sun" and "tha" means "moon." Yogis use these terms to designate two important energies that each one of us possesses. Lunar energy is feminine, emotional, intuitive, while solar energy is masculine, analytical, extroverted.

Elements of Hatha Yoga

The following are the cornerstones of yoga:

1. Physical exercises (asanas)
2. Breathing (pranayama)
3. Relaxation (shavasana, yoga nidra)
4. Positive thinking and meditation

The asanas have an effect that transcends the physical, and, particularly when poses are held for a long time and when breathing and concentration are coordinated with the poses, they influence the energy centers (chakras) and energy channels (nadis), similar to the meridians in traditional Chinese medicine (TCM). While the effects of functional gymnastics are often limited to the

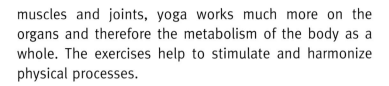

muscles and joints, yoga works much more on the organs and therefore the metabolism of the body as a whole. The exercises help to stimulate and harmonize physical processes.

Relaxation and meditation exercises prepare the body for the yoga session or accelerate the regeneration of energies after the session. They also calm the mind and harmonize energies, thus creating a holistic effect on the yoga practitioner (yogi).

Yoga Today

Both at work and at home, the pace of modern life requires us to be flexible, adaptable and dynamic, and it is constantly increasing. We are also becoming more and more specialized and sophisticated. We often neglect our own bodies in the process and only start to take notice of it if we get sick.

To stay sane in this crazy world, our desire to find a feeling of inner unity will become stronger and stronger, including the need for peace of mind and to allow the body to compensate for our sedentary lifestyles.

The held poses in yoga give us time to become aware of our own bodies. Yoga teaches us how to use our muscles effectively. By harmonizing breathing, muscle contraction and relaxing, the body is allowed to follow its own rhythm.

In the truest sense of the word, yoga offers space and time for personal development.

Please note – you should be careful of the following:

- Discuss your personal yoga program with a physician, physiotherapist or yoga teacher if you are due to have an operation in the near future or suffer from acute or chronic illnesses, from muscular wear and tear, wear a prosthesis, or have a limited range of movement.

- Avoid inverted postures if you suffer from raised blood pressure, colds or back injuries.

- If you have an acute slipped disk, avoid twisting movements or back bends.

- Pain is a warning signal that must be taken seriously. Yoga can sometimes be difficult or require great flexibility, but it should never cause you pain.

- Talk with a yoga teacher or read the appropriate specialist literature if you are pregnant.

Tips:

- Never exercise immediately after eating.

- Wear comfortable clothing.

- Depending on the exercise you are doing, use a soft, warm or non-slip mat.

- Take your time. Avoid interruptions.

- Concentrate and be mindful as you exercise. Be aware of your body. Be aware of your breathing at all times. Practice with your eyes closed as often as possible, as this encourages inner awareness.

- Use aids (chair, cushion, etc.) if you are not yet capable of doing the basic exercises.

Yoga can help you ...

Physically:

- Lower blood pressure
- Increase lung capacity
- Strengthen nerves
- Increase flexibility
- Eliminate tensions
- Relieve pain
- Improve immune defense
- Improve digestion
- Delay the signs of aging due to improved metabolism

Mentally:

- Improve concentration
- Develop greater awareness
- Become more responsible
- Develop greater flexibility

Spiritually:

- Patience
- Contentment
- Serenity
- Equilibrium
- Inner calm
- Self-confidence

YOU CAN DO IT

1 Breathing

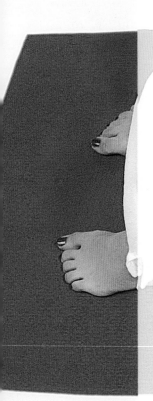

Many control systems and other internal and external factors are involved in the regulation of our breathing. The breathing pattern, i.e., its depth and frequency, changes according to how much oxygen is required by the muscles or the brain in different circumstances. Receptors in the blood and in the pulmonary alveoli sense when the supply must be increased. At rest, we breathe about 12 - 16 times per minute.

During relaxation or meditation, the breathing rate can fall to four breaths per minute, when the brain and muscles are in rest and recovery mode.

A Exercises Step by Step

Nasal Breathing

It is natural to breathe through the nose, and our breathing naturally switches between the two nostrils. Chronobiological research shows that this happens every two hours, with 80% of the air breathed in passing through the favored nostril.

Advantages of Nasal Breathing

The natural narrowing means that the air inhaled through the nose is

- cleaner,

- more moistened and

- warmer than when breathed in through the mouth.

The mucus membranes work as a filter, which is why you should always breathe in and out through your nose. The nostrils are also the location of our olfactory organs, which sense pleasant or unpleasant odors that then influence our state of mind.

If the activity level of the diaphragm is increased, e.g. ,by the increased resistance of nasal breathing, this causes other benefits, such as the promotion of venous return from the legs.

Abdominal Breathing

The downward movement of the diaphragm when inhaling compresses and stimulates the organs below. This gentle pumping action stimulates and activates the metabolism of the organs involved in the digestive process. When you breathe out, your diaphragm rises and massages your heart and also activates the vagus nerve. During the inspiration phase of deep yogic breathing, the air then flows into the abdomen. Then the movement continues over the chest and the collarbone. Breathing can become shallow, especially during exertion, i.e., in difficult or unfamiliar asanas (positions), so this is precisely when you should really try to breathe deeply but calmly.

"Relaxation Pose"

Observe your body: does your chest or your abdomen rise first when you inhale? The former is a sign of breast breathing, the latter of abdominal breathing.

Breathing and State of Mind

The way we breathe reflects our state of mind, which is why our experience of the same breathing exercises can vary from day to day.

Your state of mind is reflected in your breathing, and you can control it by controlling your breathing.

The Breathing Phases

There are three phases in the breathing process: inhalation, exhalation, and the retention of breath, the length of which depends on how relaxed you are.

If you feel unwell during the breathing exercises, or are suffering from dizziness, nausea or a headache, you should stop. If these feelings persist, stop exercising altogether. You should only perform the exercises while you are feeling well.

Lung Activation

Raise your arms to the side at head height with the palms facing upward, breathing in deeply as you do so. Fold your hands and hold your breath. Straighten your arms upward and in this state of tension lean your upper body first to the right and then to the left. Then center your body again and only then breathe out, lowering your extended arms down to the side of your body.

- With your in-breath, raise your arms and imagine that you are taking in energy.
- With your out-breath, exhale stale air and expended energy.
- Breathe in and out through your nose.

2 Gorilla

Breathe in deeply and hold your breath. Tap your lungs with your fingertips, moving outwards from your chest to your collarbone. Tap yourself from your chest downward and also tap your ribs and back. When it becomes uncomfortable to hold your breath, breathe out in bursts until your lungs are completely empty, leaning slightly forward as you do so.

Hold your breath for a moment and then breathe in deeply through your nose.

The second time around, hit your chest with a flat hand and the third time with your fist.

- Before holding your breath, inhale just enough so that it doesn't hurt when you beat your chest.
- The beating action stimulates your blood circulation, your metabolism and your lungs.
- As you hold your breath, relax your face, your neck and your larynx.

YOU CAN DO IT

Fire Reverence – Agni Sara

Inhale deeply, then breathe out and in again. Then noisily exhale as much air as possible through pursed lips, bending forward as you do so. Keep your back straight and place your hands on your thighs. Pull your stomach upward and inward. Hold your breath after exhaling. Perform a pumping movement in which you expand and contract in your stomach as quickly as possible. When you feel the need to breathe, you should do so. Breathe quickly but under control through your nose as you straighten yourself up again. Breathe out and in twice more before repeating the whole exercise 1-2 times.

This exercise gives you energy and stimulates digestion. You can increase the effect by drinking half a glass of lukewarm water before performing this exercise on an empty stomach.

Alternate Nostril Breathing – Anuloma Viloma, Nadi Shodana

4

Breathe out and in twice a little more deeply than normal to prepare yourself for this exercise. Alternately close your right nostril with your right thumb and your left nostril with your ring finger. Bend your index and ring finger. Always inhale through the same nostril through which you just exhaled, and then exhale through the other one. Count to four as you breathe out and to eight as you breathe in, in the same rhythm. Inhale and exhale about 10 times.

- Alternate nostril breathing helps you control your breathing and open your nasal passages. This breathing exercise helps to fight allergies, hay fever and asthma and prevent head colds.

- Emotional imbalances are transformed into a calm feeling of power and strength.

- Sun (active) and moon (calm) energies are harmonized.

YOU CAN DO IT

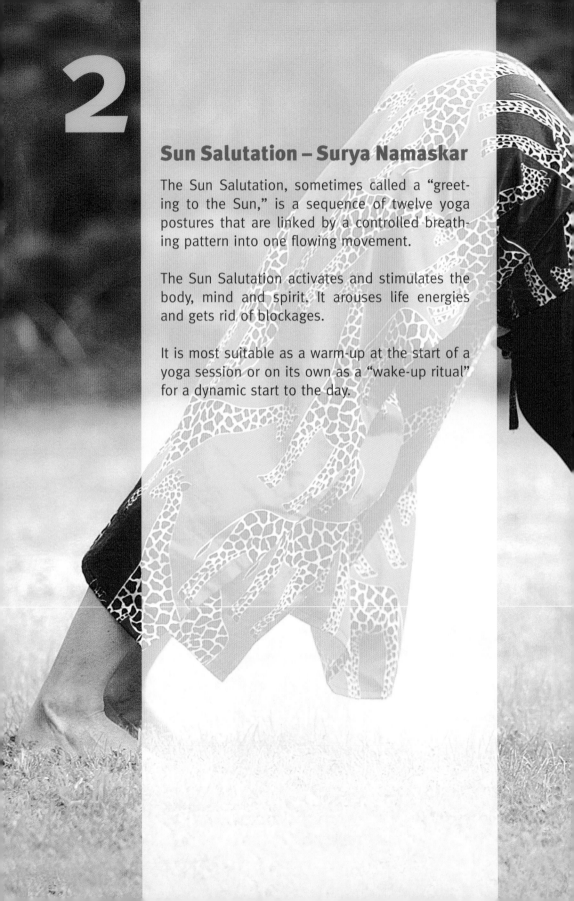

2

Sun Salutation – Surya Namaskar

The Sun Salutation, sometimes called a "greeting to the Sun," is a sequence of twelve yoga postures that are linked by a controlled breathing pattern into one flowing movement.

The Sun Salutation activates and stimulates the body, mind and spirit. It arouses life energies and gets rid of blockages.

It is most suitable as a warm-up at the start of a yoga session or on its own as a "wake-up ritual" for a dynamic start to the day.

Sun
Salutation

5

IN

EX

IN

EX

11

12

10

9

IN

8

7

EX

YOU CAN DO IT

EX

IN

1

2

EX

3

IN

4

IN = Inhale
EX = Exhale

5

Hold your Breath

6

EX

IN

One round consists of 12 poses that flow into each other. First, practice the exercises separately until you feel comfortable with them and your body knows which muscles are already tense and which can be relaxed. Then combine the exercises into a harmonious flow, aided by your breathing rhythm.

The following guidelines may be helpful:

- Inhale when you open and stretch upward or forward.

- Exhale when you bend down or look down.

The transitions and breathing pattern are described again in detail below.

In the first round, place your right leg behind you in the lunge pose and place your right leg forward coming out of the Dog Pose. In the next circuit, place your left leg to the rear and then to the front again. Swap legs in this way each time you start a new round.

As the whole sequence is very complex, start by breaking it down into individual exercises. Then carry out only exercises number 1, 2, 3, 11 and 12.

Next increase the round to include numbers 1, 2, 3, 4, 10, 11 and 12.

Finally increase again to 1, 2, 3, 4, 8, 9, 10, 11 and 12.

Practice the middle section separately:
4, 5, 6, 7, 8, 9.

Eventually combine these with the first part to form the complete Sun Salutation. First practice the movements only. Wait until you are confident in your mastery of each asana before you start to work on the correct breathing pattern.

Increase the number of circuits until you can perform about 8 - 10 circuits easily. Then start to increase the speed a little from one round to another.

This dynamic sequence is one of the few sivananda yoga exercises, which place such a demand on the cardiovascular system that you may even break into a sweat.

Pause after practicing. Open your feet hip-width apart to give you a stable base. Close your eyes and be aware of your heartbeat and your breathing.

Focus on your inhalation and exhalation. Calm your breathing by counting slowly to four as you inhale and exhale.

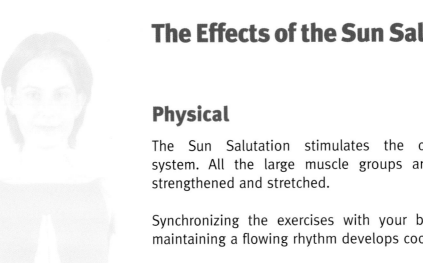

The Effects of the Sun Salutation

Physical

The Sun Salutation stimulates the cardiovascular system. All the large muscle groups are alternately strengthened and stretched.

Synchronizing the exercises with your breathing and maintaining a flowing rhythm develops coordination.

Energetic

The solar plexus is charged with energy. This energy is balanced by alternately bending forward and backward.

Mental

The Sun Salutation develops concentration. The concentration required for such a complex exercise leaves no time for thinking about the past or the future. This makes it equally suitable as both a warm-up for a yoga session and to "free your mind" in the evening after a mentally demanding day.

Take regular, deep breaths.

Om 1 Namaste, Mountain Pose

Breathe in deeply and as you breathe out, bring both hands together in front of the chest. Push your hands and your fingertips together, keeping your lower arms parallel to the floor. Your feet are close together, with your toes pointing outward for stability.

Om 2 Upward Salute

With the next inhalation, extend both arms upward. Open up your chest and lean backward so that your breastbone is facing the ceiling. Take care not to hollow your back.

Om 3 Standing Forward Bend

With your next exhalation, bend forward keeping your upper body straight. Holding your arms in line with your back is very demanding on your back. Your arms can evenly be brought down to the side. Straighten your legs as much as possible without rounding your back. Your head should hang down loosely. When your hands touch the floor, place your fingertips or the palms of your hands next to your feet, otherwise, just let your arms hang freely.

Om 4 Lunge

With your next inhalation, extend your right leg back to enter the lunge position. You can even rest your rear knee on the floor. Keep your upper body as upright as possible as you do so and face forward, even if only your fingertips are touching the floor. It is more important to keep your back straight than to put the palms of your hands on the floor.

The lower part of your front leg should be perpendicular to the floor. Make sure that your knee doesn't stick out beyond the tips of your toes. Your hips should sink as low as possible toward the floor, without your back hollowing. In the next circuit, put your left leg back instead of your right.

Om 5 Plank

Hold your breath for a moment and now extend your left leg back to enter the push-up position, so that both legs are parallel. Your upper body should be in line with your legs. If you are not strong enough to do this in the beginning, raise your hips a little. On no account should you hollow your back.

Your fingertips should point forward, and your elbows should point toward your feet.

Om 6 Staff

Now breathe out, bringing your knees, chest and forehead slowly and under control to the floor in one smooth movement.

It is easier to lower your knees first and then your upper body.

Keep your arms close to your upper body, with your shoulders pulled hard toward your feet. This avoids creating tension in your shoulders and neck. At the end of the movement, lie flat on the floor. Stretch out your feet before entering the next pose.

Om 7 Cobra

Press your hands gently into the floor. Push your fingertips away from your shoulders. Pull your hands toward your feet without moving them, thus bringing your elbows close to your body.

As you inhale, use the strength of your back to raise your upper body into the Cobra pose. Your toes are pointed and touch the floor.

Om 8 Downward Facing Dog Pose

Lower your upper body again. Press the tips of your toes down into the floor. With your next exhalation, straighten your legs and raise your hips. Straighten your arms, too. Your upper body should be in line with your arms. Keep your back as flat as possible.

Try to sink toward the floor on the outside edge of your heels.

YOU CAN DO IT

Om 9 Lunge

With your next inhalation, place your right foot (your left foot in the next circuit) between your hands once again. Look slightly in front of your hands so that your back is as flat as possible. Your fingertips or the palms of your hands touch the floor. Push your chest forward. Make sure once again that your knees remain above the tips of your toes, not in front of them.

Om 10 Standing Forward Bend

As you breathe out, place your left foot next to your right and straighten both legs as much as possible, leaning your upper body forward as you do so. Your head should now hang down loosely. When your hands touch the floor, place your fingertips or the palms of your hands next to your feet, or just let your arms hang freely. Do not round your back.

Om 11 Upward Salute

As you breathe in, raise your upper body and extend your arms upward. Open your chest, so that your breastbone is facing the ceiling. Do not hollow your back.

Om 12 Mountain Pose

As you breathe out, place your hands together in the prayer position and then let your arms hang by your side. Stand up straight and do not hollow your back.

These exercises can be performed after the initial relaxation and before the Sun Salutation. They are particularly suitable for beginners. They help to relax tense muscles. These exercises should be performed gently. Releasing tensions and performing the exercises gently are more important than being flexible. The greater your progress, the more you will be able to do of the Rishikesh Series asanas and their variations.

Preparation Exercises

Eye Exercises

Sit up straight, and relax your shoulders and neck. Ideally your forearms should rest on your legs or, if you are sitting on a chair, on a table.

With your eyes open, look alternately from right to left and back 6 times and do not focus on anything. Make this movement harmonious; try to avoid jerky movements.

Then look alternately from up to down and back 6 times, again without focusing on anything and remaining relaxed. (See the next page.)

Variations

1. Look diagonally from top right to bottom left and back and then the other diagonal, from top left to bottom right and back.

2. Roll your eyes in large circles in both directions.

3. Describe a horizontal figure 8 with your eyes.

After the eye exercises, or whenever necessary, rub your hands together hard for a moment until you can feel them getting warm. Then cup the palms of your hands over your eyes like two little caves, the darker the better. Then close your eyes. This enables your eyes and your neck muscles to relax more easily. Enjoy the pleasant sensation of warmth coming from your hands. During this resting phase, breathe in and out about 5 times. Relax more and more each time you exhale.

Effects of the Eye Exercises

Body

The eye exercises improve blood flow to the eye muscles, thereby improving eyesight. Eye exercises can also prevent headaches. The connection between eye and neck muscles means that the neck is also relaxed by the eye exercises as if it was moving gently itself. This kind of relaxation is ideal for people who spend a lot of time working in front of a computer screen and helps avoid a fixed gaze and a stiff neck.

Energy

The lunar and solar energies are harmonized.

Mind

The crossing of the middle line along the nose means that both sides of the brain are used, thus strengthening the links between the left and right hemispheres of the brain.

Mountain Pose – Tadasana

7

The Mountain Pose helps you to achieve an upright, stable and aware posture.

Stand up straight and motionless like a mountain. The insides of your ankles should be touching, but not so that there is too much pressure on the inside edge of your feet. Feel the outside edges of your feet and then press your big toe joint into the floor to produce a stable tension in the arch of your foot. Spread your toes. Because you are barefoot, your feet have plenty of room to move.

The crown of your head stretches up to the sky and your outstretched fingertips reach for the ground.

Lift your breastbone forward and upward, without hollowing your back. Pull your shoulder blades toward your spine and the bottom of your shoulder blades downward.

Breathe calmly and evenly from your abdomen. The abdominal wall should arch out gently when air flows into your lungs.

Practice this exercise often during the day whenever you have to stand. This will make you focus on ensuring your posture is correct.

Don't hold it for too long, though, for the vertebrae need to move and your muscles need a break, too.

Shoulder Relaxation

With your inhalation, pull your shoulders up toward your ears, and then lower them as you breathe out. It is important to exhale slowly. Notice how the muscles in your neck area move farther and farther away from your shoulders each time you breathe out.

Chest Opening

As you breathe in, pull both shoulders back, turning your hands outward in the process. Stretch your fingertips slightly toward the floor. Relax as you breathe out. Your shoulders and arms should only turn slightly backward as you do so. Breathe in and out several times in this position.

YOU CAN DO IT

Energy Exercise

Relax in the standing position. Close your eyes. Concentrate on your fingers; perhaps you will feel a slight prickling sensation or a pleasant feeling of warmth. Let this energy rise up your hands and arms. Feel this energy in your shoulders and up in the back of your head. Breathe calmly and evenly.

Then focus on your toes and feet. Let the energy rise from them up your legs to your pelvis and then up your back to your head.

Breathe calmly and evenly again.

Take a moment to feel this new energy rising inside you.

11 Self-Massage

Stand up straight. Twist your upper body alternately to the left and right several times, fast enough to make your arms swing. Your head should follow the movement. Your feet should be planted firmly on the floor.

Bend your rear arm slightly, so that you can tap yourself with the back of your hand on your lumbar spine/lower back. In this way, tap as much as your hand can reach of your whole lower back a little at a time. Find the places most in need of massage and enjoy the tapping massage.

The front arm swings round to the opposite side and gently taps the pelvis.

The more you relax, the easier it will be for you to twist. This exercise also mobilizes your whole spine.

YOU CAN DO IT

Lean your head gently to one side with a sigh as you breathe out and hold the position for several breaths. You can even close your eyes. Relax more each time you exhale, and let gravity work. Lift your head again as you inhale and then lean it gently to the other side and then forward. You should avoid the passive backward hyperextension of the cervical spine.

If you already have spasms, avoid the additional pulling of your head toward the floor. Your body would just react by tensing up the muscles concerned even more for protection.

13 Upright Head Posture

Place your left hand on the left side of your head and push gently. Make sure that you keep your head quite straight. Do this exercise in front of a mirror at first. Later you can close your eyes to facilitate relaxation of all other muscle areas and improve inner awareness. Take several breaths in this position. Let the tension gently fade away.

Variations

1. Push from the side with one hand and from the back with the other simultaneously.

Then push your right hand against the right side of your head, and finally push your head from behind with both hands, with interlocked fingers. Stretch your elbows out to the side and stretch out your neck. You should not feel any discomfort in your throat.

Always relax between exercises by simply shutting your eyes, standing up straight and being aware of your breathing. Each time you exhale, your tensed muscles will relax more and more.

Knee to Chest – for a relaxed lower back

Lie on your back and stretch out both legs. Feel the curvature of your lumbar spine and be aware of how your lower back feels.

Then grip your right knee and pull it toward your chest. As you breathe in, your thigh should touch your stomach, and as you breathe out, pull it closer to your chest as you relax more and more. Your left leg should be equally relaxed on the floor.

Change sides after a few breaths.

To finish, stretch out both legs again, and feel once more the curvature of your lumbar spine and your lower back. Perhaps you have already gotten rid of some tension, thus enabling your lumbar spine to sink nearer to the floor.

15 Knee Crossover - for a relaxed lower back

Cross one leg over the other and pull them both toward your chest. Hold the lower knee as firmly as possible with both hands. Breathe in with your thigh against your stomach, and as you breathe out, pull your knee closer to your chest. Relax as much as you can while you exhale.

Tip:

If you cannot lay your head down comfortably because your neck curves toward the floor, place a small cushion under your head. Relax your neck.

YOU CAN DO IT

Leg Raise - to stretch your hamstrings

As you inhale, raise your straightened left leg. Hold it as high as possible for a few breaths and then lower it as you exhale.

Then raise it once more as you inhale and this time, lower it immediately with your next exhalation. Repeat several times with your left leg.

Stretch out both legs and notice how your legs feel. Which leg feels heavier, warmer or even longer?

Then change sides.

Twisted Pose - for a supple back

Lie on your right side and bend both legs and arms. Raise your left arm and place it on your left (side) as you exhale. Let your arm fall nearer and nearer to the floor each time you exhale. Relax.

Come out of that position by taking your arm back as you inhale.

Then lie on your back before doing the exercise on the other side of your body. Notice this new sensation in your back. Perhaps you now feel as though you are lying on a slope, with one side of your body uphill and the other downhill.

Tip:

If you feel pain in your lower back or your left shoulder, pull your top knee back slightly. This will increase the twist so that it is easier for you to place your arm on the floor.

Variations

1. Stretch out your bottom leg to increase the stretch.

2. Lie on your side and cross your legs to maximize the twist and thus the mobilization of your spine. Only perform this variation if you are still able to relax in this posture.

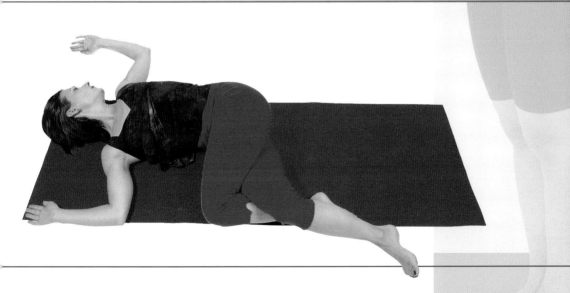

18 Abdominal Exercises - Navasana

Abdominal exercises activate the solar plexus and enhance inner balance. Their place in the exercise sequence is after the Sun Salutation and before the inverted poses.

Clasp your hands behind your head. Press your feet gently on the floor, so that your lumbar spine becomes nicely flat. Inhale deeply and then as you exhale, raise your upper body, keeping your elbows by your sides.

In this position, stretch out your head and pull your breast bone toward the ceiling. Even if you find it difficult, try to send your breath right down into your abdomen. Breathe deeply in and out several times (through your nose), and then lower your upper body back down again as you exhale and relax by stretching out your legs and arms.

YOU CAN DO IT

Variations

1. Perform the exercise as described above, but raise your legs beforehand. Bend your knees at right angles and pull your thighs gently toward your chest, not quite creating a right angle with your hips.

2. If your head doesn't need to be supported by your hands, you can also hold your arms out at your sides. This is less taxing for your abdomen, but more so for your neck muscles.

3. Raise your upper body without rounding your back. Tuck up one knee to stop yourself hollowing your back. Straighten the other leg so that it is diagonal to the ceiling if your abdominal muscles are not strong enough, or parallel to the floor if they are. Alternate these leg positions in time with your breathing: lift your straight leg as you inhale and straighten the other one as you exhale.

4. Bend your knees and hips. As you exhale, raise your upper body and turn it to the side. Hold this position and continue to breathe calmly and evenly through your nose. Rest a while before working the other side.

YOU CAN DO IT

The Wave

19

The Wave is a complex exercise that consists of a sequence of 4 movements, and therefore 4 breaths (2 inhalations, 2 exhalations).

1. With your first inhalation, press both elbows down into the floor without hollowing your back.

2. With your next exhalation, roll your chin onto your chest. The idea is to stretch the back of your neck as much as possible and to lower your collarbone. Pull your elbows together. This is not an abdominal exercise; so only raise your head slightly.

3. With your next inhalation, raise your pelvis as you lower your head and your elbows.

4. With your last exhalation, unroll your spine, vertebra by vertebra and lay back down on the floor.

This exercise sequence supples and relaxes your back.

So that you can hear your tensions, hum "mmmm" as you uncurl your spine in step 4. Listen carefully. Do you hear a continuous humming or are there a few jerks or even breaks?

Repeat the whole exercise sequence several times until the humming sounds continuous and even.

YOU CAN DO IT

4 The Rishikesh Series

The Rishikesh Series consists of the initial relaxation pose, breathing and warm-up exercises (e.g., the Sun Salutation), the 12 basic poses and the final relaxation pose. The basic exercises are described in this chapter, along with some variations.

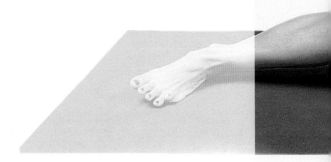

There are inverted poses, forward bends, backbends and twisted poses. These four categories should be practiced in every yoga session in the above order. Depending on your experience and physical fitness, you can then select more exercises from each category or simplify or vary the exercises as required.

As you perform the exercises, bear in mind the following basic principles:

- Make sure that you perform the exercise correctly, i.e., contract only where required; relax all other muscles.

- Go with your body's feelings and accept your own limitations. Yoga exercises should never be painful.

- Aim for relaxed, abdominal breathing and if you can, use Ujjayi, (see chapter on relaxation), so that you can slip further into the end position.

- Focus your mind on performing the exercise and on your breathing. It is easier to be in tune with yourself if you close your eyes. Forget all thoughts of the past and future and stay in the present moment.

Shoulderstand - Sarvagasana

20

Begin the Shoulderstand lying on your back. Bend your legs and then straighten them with an upward push as you breathe in. Keep your legs together. Support your back with your hands. Bring your elbows as close together as possible and push them against the floor to take the pressure off your spine. When your little fingers are touching, you know that your hands are the same height. Relax your feet and calves. You should have a feeling of space around your throat and your lower jaw should be relaxed. Make sure that your head is in line with your spine. To come out of this position, first move your legs slightly toward your head and then smoothly unroll your spine.

Effects

The Shoulderstand is particularly effective as a way of resting and revitalizing after a stressful day.

Being upside down stimulates the venous return from the legs and helps to prevent varicose veins. The digestive tract is also stimulated, which also helps avoid stomach problems. Added benefits are the normalization of thyroid function and an improved blood supply to the entire head area.

Variations

If you are not strong enough to perform a Shoulderstand with vertical legs, start off with a diagonal position. Support your pelvis with your hands. This doesn't require much strength when your forearms are vertical. Keep your elbows as close together as possible. Relax your legs. Keep your back straight.

YOU CAN DO IT

You can also rest your arms on a plump cushion.

Advanced beginners can also go from the vertical Shoulderstand described above into a half-Lotus position by bending one leg and turning it out at the hip.

Please Note...

Be careful if you have very high blood pressure or an inflammation (sinus, teeth, ears).

Avoid the Shoulderstand if you have degenerative or inflammatory wear and tear in your cervical spine, raised intra-ocular pressure or cataracts, or suffer from detached retina.

21 Plow - Halasana

With your exhalation, lower one leg from the Shoulder-stand to the floor and then raise it again with your next inhalation.

Repeat the exercise with the other leg. If you are in good enough shape to lower both legs together easily, do it. You are always a little less flexible in the morning than in the evening.

Press your forearms into the floor. If you are sufficiently flexible, do it with your hands clasped. You should have a feeling of space in your throat region and your lower jaw should be relaxed. Straighten your back, by trying to hollow your back. Don't worry, you will not be able to do so in this position. Pull back your toes and straighten your legs to further intensify the stretch. To exit this position, place your hands on the floor to act as brakes and smoothly unroll your back as you breathe out.

Effects

Like the Shoulderstand, the Plow harmonizes thyroid function, and the abdominal organs also receive a gentle massage. In addition, the strong stretch rids the back and your neck of tensions.

Variations

If your feet do not reach the floor, you can leave them hanging in the air. If you cannot relax sufficiently in this position, rest your feet on a plump cushion or a chair. Stretch out your spine and legs each time you inhale, and relax each time you exhale, without changing your position.

Please note

Be careful if you have very high blood pressure or an inflammation (sinus, teeth, ears).

Avoid the Plow if you have symptoms of degenerative or inflammatory wear and tear in your cervical spine, raised intra-ocular pressure or cataracts, or suffer from detached retina.

22

Bridge - Setu Bandhasana

The Bridge and the Fish (see next exercise) are back bends and therefore are counter postures to the Shoulderstand and the Plow and should be carried out after them.

YOU CAN DO IT

You can either go directly out of the Shoulderstand into the Bridge or begin the Bridge separately.

Support your lower back with your hands. Place your feet shoulder-width apart or closer. Pull your knees forward, but no further forward than your toes. This will stretch your spine and avoid compression in your back.

Effects

The Bridge has a regenerative effect. It strengthens the whole back area, gently stretches the back of your neck and the front of your body. It leads to a feeling of harmony and unity.

Variations

These variations are only for the very flexible.

Straighten your legs completely, keeping the soles of both feet on the floor. Both the inside and outside edges of your feet should bear your weight. Do not open either your elbows or your knees wider than in the basic position.

Place your heels on your fingertips. Continue to stretch your spine.

Grip your ankles with your hands. Only perform this variation if you can still stretch your back at the same time, by pulling your knees forward (but no further forward than your toes). In this variation, too, both the inside and outside edges of your feet should bear your weight.

Please note!

Be careful if you have very high blood pressure or inflammation (sinus, teeth, ear). Avoid the Bridge if you have symptoms of degenerative or inflammatory wear in your cervical spine, raised intra-ocular pressure or cataracts, or suffer from detached retina.

YOU CAN DO IT

The Fish and the Bridge (see previous exercise) are back bends and as such are counter postures to the Shoulderstand and the Plow. They should therefore be carried out after the latter to compensate.

Place your arms close together under your back. Then, as you breathe in, engage your elbows and raise your upper body. Stretch your whole spine; your breastbone should point toward the ceiling. Now lower your head to the floor. Make sure that your head is not bearing too much weight. Support your upper body with your elbows and as your back gets stronger, it will eventually be able to bear most of the weight of your upper body. Concentrate mainly on using the strength in your upper back by pulling both shoulder blades toward your spine and arching your sternum upward. Breathe deeply and evenly in your abdomen and chest. Relax your legs.

To exit this position, engage your elbows as you breathe in and raise your head again, if possible, far enough so that you can see the tips of your toes. Then lay your upper body back on the floor as you breathe out.

Effects

The Fish also harmonizes the function of the thyroid and helps alleviate tense shoulder and neck muscles that were perhaps painful during the Shoulderstand. The Fish is good for correcting round shoulders. It particularly strengthens the muscles in the chest and lumbar spine. The chest is expanded to allow you to breathe deeply. Emotional tensions can be released.

Variations

If you cannot lay your head on the mat, keep it in the air. As this can make the exercise more difficult to do, especially if you are still looking at the ceiling, do not hold the position for too long.

You can also place a plump cushion under your back to help you to open up your chest. You can lie almost passively on the cushion in this position. In order to progress in this asana, you should try to develop strength in your upper back in spite of the cushion.

Please note

Be careful if you have problems with your shoulders or your cervical spine.

Place a cushion under your head if you suffer from very high blood pressure or a hyperactive thyroid.

24

Forward Bend - Paschimothanasana

Sit up straight with your feet in front of you and pull both buttocks back with your hands, so that your pelvis is pushed as far forward as possible. Hold the stretch in both legs. As you inhale, raise both arms and as you exhale, bend forward from your hips, keeping your back straight. Then let your arms hang loosely. Each time you inhale, stretch your head up higher and higher and as you exhale, relax your hips and the backs of your thighs, so that eventually you may be able to come down a little further. Try to bring your navel toward your legs.

Then try to relax for several breaths as you lay your upper body on your knees.

Avoid rounding your back under any circumstances. The exercise will then do you more harm than good.

Effects

The Forward Bend stimulates the immune system and can be helpful if you feel you are getting a cold. It also stimulates the abdominal organs, e.g., the kidneys, liver and the pancreas (good for diabetics) and stretches your hamstrings and calves.

Variations

Bend one leg to the side. The foot touches the other thigh. Bend forward at the hips keeping your back straight.

If your upper body cannot lie comfortably on your knees, use a cushion or a chair to help you.

To start with, just sitting up straight can stretch your hamstrings sufficiently. Support yourself by placing your hands right behind your bottom on the floor.

Tip 1:

Place a blanket under your bottom to make it easier to tip your pelvis forward.

Tip 2:

If you cannot reach your feet with your hands, place a belt around the balls of your feet as an extension of your arms and do the belt up. Pull yourself forward keeping your back straight.

Please note

Use aids to help you if you have a very rounded back. You should then concentrate more on stretching than on relaxing.

If you have sciatic problems (due to symptoms of degenerative wear and tear or a slipped disk), avoid stretching until you feel pain.

Be careful in the case of inflammations or recent abdominal operations.

YOU CAN DO IT

Inclined Plane - Purvotthasana

25

This is also called the Staff Pose – Caturanga Dandasana.

The Inclined Plane is a counter posture to the Forward Bend, and should therefore be performed after it.

Sit up straight and then push up into the Staff pose. Stretch both your pelvis and your breastbone up as high as possible. You can touch your toes with your fingers, or let them point away from your feet. Make sure that your elbows are not hyperextended. Lift your pelvis high, while at the same time pushing it toward your feet. This makes it easier to put your feet on the floor. This pose requires a lot of strength, but you should breathe calmly and evenly nonetheless.

Wrong!

Do not let your shoulders hang passively. Do not hyperextend your elbows.

Effects

Strengthens the entire trunk supporting musculature. Stimulates the circulation and deepens breathing. Improves stamina.

Variations

If you are still not sufficiently strong to push yourself up high enough to be able to look at the ceiling, do not hyperextend your cervical spine in an attempt to look up. Just look straight ahead. Push yourself as far as possible "out of" your shoulders

Tip:

By contracting your pelvic floor muscles, your pelvis can stretch even higher.

YOU CAN DO IT

The "Table" is an easier variation of the Inclined Plane, in which you bend your knees to take the pressure off your lower back. Do not let the angle of your knees be less than 90°. Stretch your hips as far as possible.
Your head can be extended still further, or even bent in the case of cervical spine problems.

Please note

Take care if you have wrist problems and support yourself on your fists instead. This can make the posture more unstable, so be careful.

Treat your body gently if you feel a little below par. This posture requires a great deal of strength.

26 Cobra - Bhujangasana

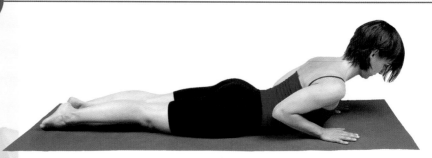

Lie on your stomach with your hands under your shoulders, so that your fingertips are level with your shoulders. Stretch your feet and contract your buttocks. Pull your hands toward your feet, but without visible movement. This stretches your spine, which is a basic prerequisite for every back bend. It makes it easier if you push your breastbone forward. Place your elbows close to your trunk and lower your shoulders.

Then use the strength of your back to push upward. The important thing is not to look up, but for your sternum to push away from your upper back. Check that your elbows stay close to the sides of your trunk and that your shoulders are lowered. Otherwise, tension could build up in the back of your neck.

Wrong!

YOU CAN DO IT

Don't let the upward push only come from your arms; it should come mainly from the strength of your back. Place your hands under your shoulders, not in front of them. The back bend comes from your upper back, not only from your cervical spine. Never bring your head back if you have very rounded shoulders.

Effects

The pressure on the abdominal organs from the abdominal breathing helps counteract constipation and menstrual pain. The entire back is strengthened. The front of the trunk is stretched and the breathing is deepened. The Cobra has a generally activating effect.

Variations

You can perform the Cobra even higher. From time to time, check how much strength is actually coming from your back by lifting your hands for a few breaths.

Please note

Be careful if you have acute problems in the lumbar spine area, and only raise your upper body a few centimeters from the floor.

27

Locust - Shalabhasana

Fold your hands and stick your thumbs up. Alternatively, you can make your hands into fists and push them next to each other under your pelvis. Then lay your straight arms as close together as possible under your pelvis and pull them toward your feet. Gather your strength in your arms and as you inhale, raise your legs, keeping them straight and as close together as possible. Develop the strength from your back and at the same time push your arms down into the floor.

Take several breaths in this position and then slowly lower your legs back to the floor.

YOU CAN DO IT

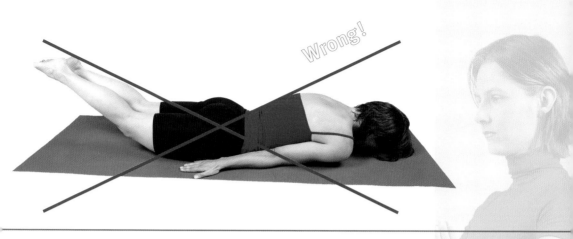

Wrong!

For a variation that protects the back of the neck, you can put your forehead on the floor, but only if you avoid rounding your shoulders. Keep your back as flat as possible. You may only be able to lift your legs a few centimeters off the ground in your first attempts. You will still feel the positive effects though. It is better to raise your legs a little less high, but to hold them for a few breaths longer.

Effects

The function of the intestines is strengthened. The liver, pancreas and kidneys are massaged. Bottom and back muscles are strengthened. This asana also improves willpower and stamina.

Variations

If you don't have the strength to raise both legs to start with, raise just one. You can also choose a more comfortable hand position. Place your hands at the side of your trunk on the floor. Keep your back as flat as possible by pushing your chin forward.

Another variation consists of supporting the raised leg with your other leg. Although this requires less strength, it develops flexibility. Stretch your lower back in particular, to avoid squashing your spine.

YOU CAN DO IT

The Bird is a variation of the Locust, which also involves raising the arms behind you. The height of your arms and legs depends on the strength and flexibility of your shoulders and lower back.

Please note

If you feel acute pain in your lower back, choose the easier variations of the Locust or avoid the exercise completely.

You should also be careful if you have acute inflammation of the abdomen.

28

Cat - Majariasana

The Cat is a separate asana, but it can also be performed as an easy variation of the Locust.

On your hands and knees, lower your breastbone to the floor as you inhale, and push it gently toward the front edge of the mat. As you do so, raise your head slightly, without shortening the back of your neck. Do not hollow your back.

As you exhale, arch your lower back toward the floor. Do not hollow your back. It is easy to round your shoulders, but that is not the point of this posture. Bring your chin toward your breastbone.

Effects

The Cat mobilizes and strengthens all sections of the spine.

Variations

As you inhale, raise one leg to the rear. As you exhale, pull the knee underneath your stomach.

You can also extend the diagonally opposite arm and pull it toward your knee.

29

Bow - Dhanurasana

Lie on your stomach and stretch out your spine. In this position, grip your ankles with your hands, having bent your legs toward your bottom. Hold the spinal stretch for as long as possible. Then simultaneously lift your upper body and your legs from the floor. Push your feet into your hands to enable you to lift your thighs higher. Keep your shoulders as low as possible to avoid tensing your neck.

Effects

Strengthens your back and buttock muscles. Stretches the front of your body. This is a good counter posture to the seated postures. Massages the abdominal organs, which helps ward off constipation and other stomach-intestinal disorders. an gets rid of congestion in the abdominal area.

Variations

An easier variation is initially to only grip one ankle with the hand on the same side of your body. Place the other lower arm on the floor and pull it toward your feet. The spine stretches and the breastbone points forward and upward.

In the Rocking Bow, a little rocking movement is performed in time with the breathing. As you inhale, consciously stretch out your stomach. This will make your upper body even straighter. When you relax your stomach as you exhale, your upper body will lower again slightly. Use this movement to stretch your legs even higher to counterbalance.

Please note

If you have acute lumbar spine problems, if possible, compensate for the Bow by following it with a half Locust or a gentle, flat Cobra.

Be careful if you have stomach complaints or a hyperactive thyroid.

After this asana, relax in the Pose of the Child (see Relaxation chapter).

Start off by sitting on your heels. Then slide your bottom to the left of your feet. Cross over your right leg and put your right foot to the left of your left leg. Make sure that both buttocks remain on the floor. If necessary, pull your left foot out a little. Hold your right leg firmly with both hands and straighten your spine as much as possible. Inhale and stretch your right arm up. Twist your upper body to the right as you exhale and place your right hand right under your bottom. Straighten up your spine again. Bring your left elbow behind your knee and grip your ankle, raising your left shoulder in the process.

Each time you inhale, stretch upward again and then relax as you exhale, without altering your position. As you relax, twist a little more into the position. Inhale with your abdomen against your thigh. This gives your abdominal organs a little extra massage.

To come out of this position, raise your right, rear arm as you inhale. As you exhale, twist forward again with your straightened spine. Then change sides.

Don't turn your right shoulder in. Turn your hand out. Don't round your shoulders. Stretch your sternum out in the twisted position. Don't just let your right shoulder droop; lower both shoulders actively. Pull the leg of the foot that is resting on the floor toward you. Don't let your left leg turn out. Point your toes toward the ceiling.

Effects

The small rotary back muscles are strengthened by the active position. This prevents back pain and also provides emergency relief for pain caused by sitting down for too long.

This asana strengthens the sympathetic nervous system and generally alleviates nervous complaints. It helps to get rid of stress. Also, the gentle abdominal massage helps to eliminate toxins produced during the digestive process.

Variations

In case that the twist does not go very far or the stomach is in the way (overweight, pregnant), then it is an easier variation when you twist toward the open side.

To do this, turn your left leg out, straighten your right leg and turn right. Push your left elbow against your left knee. Do not let your left knee sag.

Sit up straight and pull your right leg toward you and place your foot on the floor to the left of your left thigh. Then twist into the position, as described in the basic exercise. Extend your right arm without raising your shoulder. Keep your spine as vertical as possible. Turn your head in the direction of movement. Place your left arm on your right leg and pull it in toward your trunk. Stretch the inside edge of your left foot away. Sit on both buttocks.

Perform the Spinal Twist while sitting on your heels. This variation is a little more difficult, as the twist comes from the strength of your back. Keep your hands by your sides, pull your elbows back. Roll with your bottom on your feet until your back is no longer hollow. Then, as you exhale, twist your upper body round. In the final position, your shoulders and elbows should be the same height. Pull your elbows back once more. Make sure that you do not hollow your back.

Please note

Do not perform twisting movements if you suffer from severely damaged vertebral disks or acute sciatica. Be careful if you are suffering from stomach problems.

YOU CAN DO IT

Crow - Kakasana

This asana develops strength and balance. Assume a squatting position with your legs apart. Place your hands in front of you on the mat so that your knees fit under your armpits. Your knees can also be turned out slightly so that they rest on your upper arms. Then straighten your legs and shift your weight onto your hands. When all the weight is transferred from your legs, raise them and bring your feet together. Look straight ahead, not down. This exercise requires some practice. Try it calmly several times in succession.

Effects

The Crow improves coordination and balance and strengthens the arms and shoulder and chest musculature. It has an activating effect and prevents nervous problems. The Crow helps you to develop courage, concentration and willpower.

Variations

You can place a plump cushion on the floor in front of your head in case you lose your balance and fall over forward. You can even hold the pose if you fall.

Please note

Be careful if you have weak wrists.

Standing Forward Bend - Pada Hastasana

The classic Standing Forward Bend is performed with the legs together. As very flexible hamstrings are required to bend forward a long way, or a very strong back is needed to hold the pose with your back flat, here it is recommended the variation be done with the legs apart. Make sure your body weight is loaded equally on both the inside and outside edges of your feet.

Breathe in and stretch both arms into the air. With your next exhalation, lower your upper body, keeping your back straight. Bend from your hips, i.e., your navel leads the movement. Try to relax once you are in the final position. Stretch the crown of your head even further with your next inhalation and relax as you breathe out, while bending a little further forward. Keep your head in line with your spine.

If you are able to bend forward a long way, fold your arms and grip your elbows.

YOU CAN DO IT

If you cannot bend for-
ward very far, and can-
not relax with your back
straight, do the variation
with a chair.

Don't bend forward from
your back, as this encourages you to round your
back. Bend from your
hips and pull your navel
toward the floor.

Effects

The hamstrings are
strongly stretched, which
counteracts long hours
of sitting at a desk. It
takes the pressure off

the vertebrae, because they are no longer bearing all
the weight of the upper body. The blood supply to the
brain is stimulated. The Standing Forward Bend therefore has some of the positive effects of the Twisting
postures, and is invigorating and energizing.

Variations

Use a chair back, a windowsill or a table
that is the right height for your own level
of flexibility. Each time you inhale, stretch
out your spine and as you exhale, relax,
letting your breastbone fall toward the
floor in the process. Avoid hollowing your
back. For this variation, your legs don't
need to be so far apart.

Fold your arms. Keep your spine straight. In the final position, shift your body weight as far back as possible so that you feel more weight on your heels. Take several breaths in this position. Then transfer your weight forward onto the balls of your feet. Take several breaths in this position also. Alternate backward and forward several times and feel how the stretch changes in your legs. With time, you will be able to bend further and further forward.

YOU CAN DO IT

If you are very flexible and can already bend forward a long way, grip your ankles with your hands and pull your chest nearer to your legs. This also strengthens your upper back, which prevents round shoulders. You can press your head against the floor or a plump cushion.

Please note

Use equipment if you are very round-shouldered or suffer from sciatica (due to symptoms of degenerative wear and tear or a slipped disk). In this case, you should take more care when stretching than when relaxing. Avoid this pose if it becomes painful.

33

Tree - Vrikhasana

Stand up straight and still. Contract the arches of your feet. Put the palms of your hands together. Pressing them together lightly gives you stability. Keep your forearms parallel to the floor. Then lift one leg and place the foot against your thigh. Apply light pressure and counter-pressure. Straighten your support leg. Compensate for slight wobbles with the muscles of your foot and not with your knee. Actively push the balls of your feet and your heels down into the floor.

Stare at a fixed object in front of you. After several deep breaths, change sides.

YOU CAN DO IT

Wrong!

Do not hollow your back. Tip your pelvis forward. Contract your gluteal muscles.

Effects

The Tree is good training for the arches of your feet and therefore prevents an incorrect gait. The stronger the arches of your feet are, the more stable you will be.

The Tree improves your sense of balance and your stability.

Variations

The height of your leg is not so important in the beginning. To start with, you can rest your foot against the back of your other foot, against your ankle, your calf or your knee. First find your balance.

If you already have good balance and would like to improve your hip flexibility, place your foot in the half-Lotus position on the opposite thigh.

Please note

Stand near something on which you can support yourself if you suffer from dizziness or low blood pressure.

YOU CAN DO IT

Standing Balance – Utthita Satyeshikasana

34

The Standing Balance is one of a group of balancing asanas and also a preparation for many other standing postures.

From a standing position, dynamically thrust both arms up. Contract the arches of your feet. Lean your upper body forward as you raise your right leg. Hold your arms in line with the raised leg. If possible, bend until your upper body is horizontal. Do not twist your right hip. Each time you inhale, try to lean forward a little more. Relax as you exhale, without changing position. Inhale as you stand up straight again and then change sides.

Effects

Strengthens the entire back of your body, your support leg and support foot. Stimulates the circulation and breathing. Improves sense of balance.

Variations

Do not bend until your upper body is horizontal, but keep your arms and legs in a diagonal position. Your arms and the raised leg form a line. This does not require as much strength as the basic exercise, and you can put your foot on the floor more quickly if you feel you are losing your balance.

Please note

Be careful if you suffer from high blood pressure or still feel generally weak, e.g., after a cold.

YOU CAN DO IT

Triangle - Trikonasana

Stand with your feet a little more than hip-width apart for stability. As you inhale, raise your left arm and then lower your upper body and right arm to the right as you exhale. Push your left foot hard into the floor in order to keep your pelvis centered. Keep your pelvis tipped forward, as it was in the standing position. Stretch the top of your trunk. You may place your right hand on your leg. Try not to support yourself too much with it, and use the strength of your back muscles instead. Each time you inhale, stretch your back by pulling the right side of your trunk to the floor and then relax as you exhale and lower yourself a little near the floor, without rounding your back.

After several deep breaths, change sides.

Effects

The Triangle posture stimulates the appetite and aids digestion. It strengthens the small and large back extensor muscles, thus preventing back pain. It stretches the latissimus dorsi, this preventing a hollow back. It also strengthens the leg and hip muscles.

The liver is massaged, thus stimulating bile flow. Breathing in the lateral dimension is strengthened. This asana will also improve your balance.

You see the world from another angle, which makes you open to new things in your life.

Variations

This variation makes the small rotator muscles of the back extensors work even harder. Open your legs wider than for the basic exercise (4 - 5 feet). Turn your right foot out at 90° and the left foot inward a little. Raise both arms until they are horizontal. Then push your upper body to the right until you can no longer hold your arms horizontally. Then bring your right arm down and your left arm up. Twist the left side of your pelvis round and backward as far as possible. Support yourself with your right hand on the floor, on your leg or, if necessary, on a stool. Keep both sides of your trunk the same length.

YOU CAN DO IT

Breathing is the same as in the basic exercise.

Place your legs exactly as in the previous exercise, but turn your upper body backward. In this exercise, you should also rest your hand on the floor or some other support surface. It can also be placed on the outside of the right leg or on the back of your foot. Stretch your spine. Load your body weight onto the outside edge of your rear leg foot.

The Hero Triangle is another version of the triangle posture, for which you should bend your right leg, if possible until your thigh is horizontal. Take your left arm above your head so that it forms a line with your left leg. Look straight ahead, and if the muscles in the back of your neck are strong enough, upward. Each time you inhale, stretch your spine, and relax as you exhale, without changing the position. To come out of the asana, bring your arm back a little in the other diagonal, so that as you inhale, your arm pulls you out of the position.

Please note

Avoid this exercise if you suffer from acute disk damage or sciatica. Be careful if you have a stomach illness.

YOU CAN DO IT

5

A relaxation phase at the beginning and end of the yoga session helps to regenerate energy, thereby enabling you to recover from your daily stress or the preceding yoga session.

During deep relaxation, stress hormones are broken down and happiness hormones are released. The vegetative nervous system switches from active (sympathetic nervous system) to relaxation (parasympathetic nervous system). The cardiovascular system slows down, enabling the prevention of diseases like high blood pressure, stomachaches, digestive problems, headaches and colds.

You should not go to sleep during relaxation. Your mind should remain awake. When you learn to relax, it will help you in your daily life and also to get to sleep more quickly. When you go to sleep feeling relaxed and your mind is calm, you will wake up in the morning feeling refreshed and full of energy.

Our minds are constantly busy going over past events or planning for the future.

In order to relax physically, our minds have to be calm. The best way to achieve this is to concentrate on the present. Your breathing is a good place to start.

Be patient with yourself.

Relaxation

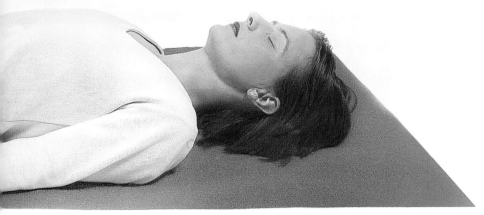

36

Focused Breathing

Abdominal breathing is the breathing of relaxation. Feel how your abdomen rises gently when you inhale and then lowers as you exhale.

Count to four when you inhale and to four when you exhale. Try not to force it. The more relaxed you are, the calmer your breathing will be.

When you notice that you are slowly becoming relaxed, count to four as you inhale and to eight as you exhale. The counting and breathing should be in harmony with each other. Do not put pressure on yourself by counting too fast or too slowly.

37

Ujjayi

By closing the glottis, your breath can flow slowly and under control.

You can achieve this by whispering with an aspirate "Haaa" to start with. Do this several times to learn how to do Ujjayi.

Now close your mouth and breathe through your nose. Then "say" the word "Haaaa" as you exhale, but without voicing it. There should be a faint noise. Try to breathe like this without forcing. If you make snoring noises as you practice, you are on the right track, you just have to do it unvoiced and not force it.

You can use this breathing technique during the whole yoga session, if it isn't too tiring, and also during your daily life when you want to relax. The slow, controlled exhaling is enough by itself to make you relax.

Relaxation Poses

Standing Relaxation

As a quick relaxation break between asanas (poses), you can also relax standing up. Stand with your legs hip-width apart for stability position. If you have a good sense of balance, you can even stand with your feet together. Feel both the outer and inner edges of your feet. Avoid hollowing your back by keeping your pelvis tilted. Lift your breastbone forward and upward without forcing. Continue to breathe using abdominal relaxation breathing (see Breathing chapter).

Corpse Pose - Shavasana

Push your buttocks toward your feet with your hands to bring your lumbar spine nearer the floor so that it can relax. Stretch out the back of your neck. Turn the palms of your hands up and push your shoulder blades like two small cushions toward your spine and lower your shoulders to the floor in the direction of your feet. Relax your hips so that your feet fall outward. When you are in bed, make sure that the blankets don't restrict your feet. Relax with your eyes shut.

Cross-Legged Seated Poses

You can relax, meditate and do breathing exercises in the sitting position.

To make it easier to keep your pelvis, and therefore also your spine, straight, it is advisable to put a cushion or a rolled-up blanket underneath your bottom.

You can sit in the Tailor posture (sukhasana) or place one foot in front of the other (muktasana).

Relax your hips and let your knees sink to the floor. If your knees do not touch the floor, you can also put a cushion under them to take the load off your hips. Don't forget to put the other leg forward, as well.

Let your head reach upward, but keep your pelvis firmly on the floor or cushion.

Form a circle by placing the thumb and index finger of one hand together. This hand position (mudra) enables energy to flow. If it is easy to keep your upper body upright, place your hands with the palms up, or if this position causes you to tense up, palms down.

YOU CAN DO IT

If you have very flexible hips, you can sit in the Lotus position (padmasana) or in the half Lotus position (ardha padmasana). For this, you place one or both feet on the top of your thighs in the groin area. Only sit in the Lotus position if your hips are flexible enough that you can comfortably lower both knees to the floor.

Keep your pelvis in a central position. Do not hollow your back or hold it too far back. Sit up as straight as possible and, from time to time, make sure that you are still stretching upward. If you don't do this, gravity will quickly make you sag.

Tip:

Let the movement come from your hips and not from your knees, as otherwise your knees will be damaged.

41

Pose of a Child - Garbhasana

This position is also known as the Embryo position. Sit on your heels, then stretch forward your arms and your whole back.

If you can comfortably lay your forehead on the floor without feeling pain in your cervical spine, place your arms at the side of your body, with the palms of your hands facing the ceiling. Notice how your abdomen arches against your thigh as you inhale. Close your eyes and relax all your muscles and your mind, too. It is a good idea to perform this position in-between or after the back bends, as it is a great way to relax and stretch your back.

Tip:

To avoid rounding your back, just open your knees to allow your trunk to fit comfortably between them.

YOU CAN DO IT

Reversed Corpse Pose

42

Lay your head on your forearms, so that the back of your neck is stretched and your nose has room to breathe.

Place your feet either so that your big toes are touching and your heels fall outward, or they are so far from each other that the heels can fall inward and the tips of your toes point outward.

Tip:

If you cannot relax with your head upright, lay it to one side, on your forearms or directly on the mat. Make sure that you lay your head on the other side next time.

43 Yawning Exercise

YOU CAN DO IT

Lie comfortably on your back. Close your eyes. Raise your arms above your head and lay them on the floor as you inhale.

Grip your right knee as you exhale deeply, raising your entire upper body and rounding your back. Pull your chin toward your chest to stretch the back of your neck. Wait calmly in this position until you feel the need to inhale. This can take a few seconds.

As you inhale, you will feel a strong need to yawn. Surrender to this feeling and yawn heartily and deeply. As you do so, come out of the position and stretch your arms above your head again and lay your upper body back down on the floor and relax.

When you exhale again while yawning, bring your arms back down by your side to the starting position.

Swap the knee that you grip before yawning, first the right and then the left. Notice how you feel more and more relaxed each time you yawn.

44 Initial Relaxation

Perform the Initial Relaxation right at the start of your yoga session.

Close your eyes and lie comfortably on your back (see relaxation positions).

Go over in your mind the events of the day.

What positive things have you done today?

Maybe you have done something that you had been planning for a long time. Also think about the little things in life.

What has brought you joy? Have you finished a project? Have you enjoyed meeting nice people? Colleagues, friends or family? Did something good happen today?

Then remember the preparations that you have made for this exercise sequence.

YOU CAN DO IT

In your mind, shut the door to this space.

Enjoy the calm, relaxation, awareness of your body and focused breathing. Enjoy having time for yourself.

Be consciously aware of your breathing and do Ujjayi breathing (see "Focused Breathing" in this chapter and "Ujjayi Breathing").

Then feel your body from the top of your head to the tips of your toes. Feel which parts of your body are touching the floor. Push down on the floor in these places. You should have the feeling that you are sinking deeper and deeper into the floor and are being swallowed up by the earth.

Feel heaviness or lightness. Happiness and warmth. Let everything go and be full of confidence.

Feel the slight curvature of your lumbar spine – your shoulders – your shoulder blades – your arms and hands. In your mind, continue on to your trunk. Feel how your shoulders narrow into your waist. Feel how your lumbar spine is slightly raised from the floor. Notice your pelvis – your hips – your thighs – the curvature of the backs of your knees – and your feet.

Relax all your muscles. Relax completely.

Practice being aware of your breathing, your body and your mind.

45 Final Relaxation

Perform this final relaxation at the end of your yoga session. It should be part of every warm-down, even if you have little time available.

Lie in the Back Relaxation position.

Pull the tip of your right foot up toward your knee. Raise your straightened right leg a few centimeters from the floor. Hold the contraction. Feel the tension in your right shin, thigh and hip, then relax. Lower your leg gently back to the floor, and notice which muscles relax as you do so.

Then pull the toes of your left foot toward your knee. Raise your straightened left leg a few centimeters from the floor. Hold the contraction. Feel the tension in your left shin, thigh and hip, then relax. Lower your leg gently back to the floor, again, notice which muscles relax as you do so.

Contract your bottom. Clench your buttocks firmly together so that your entire pelvis curves away from the floor slightly. Hold the contraction. Feel the tension in your bottom, then relax. Lower your pelvis gently back to the floor.

After every contraction, notice which muscles relax.

Now firmly tense your abdomen, so that your lumbar spine approaches the floor. If you still cannot touch it,

YOU CAN DO IT

dig your heels into the floor. Hold the contraction. Feel the tension in your abdomen. Keep breathing calmly and evenly. Then relax and feel how your abdomen starts to following the breathing motion again.

Contract your upper back by pulling your shoulder blades in toward your spine. Narrow your shoulders and feel how your whole chest curves up to the ceiling. Then relax again.

Make both hands up into fists and raise both arms a few centimeters from the floor. Hold the contraction. Feel the tension in your hands, arms and shoulders. Then relax again.

Immediately stretch out your fingers and hands, with your thumbs pointing upward. Press the palms of both hands against the floor and pull your shoulders toward your feet. Hold the contraction, and feel it in your hands, arm and upper back. Then relax again.

Push the back of your head gently against the mat. Hold the contraction. Feel the tension in the back of your neck. Then relax again.

Make a face like you are tasting a bitter lemon. Pull all your muscles toward the tip of your nose. Wrinkles are formed everywhere, on your forehead, cheeks and chin. Feel how your whole face is tensed. Then relax again.

Then make a Lion face. Open your eyes wide and look up over your eyebrows toward your forehead. Open your mouth really wide and stretch your tongue right

down to your chin. Lift your head a few centimeters from the floor. Hold this tension. Lay your head down again with a sigh and relax all your muscles. Close your eyes and mouth.

Turn your head to the right again as you exhale. As you inhale, bring it back to the center again and turn it to the left next time you exhale, and then back to the center once more as you inhale. Stretch out the back of your neck again and find a comfortable position.

Go over all the parts of your body in your mind, and say the following sentences to yourself:

"I relax my right foot, my right foot is completely relaxed.

I relax my right calf, my right calf is completely relaxed.

YOU CAN DO IT

I **relax** my right thigh, my right thigh is completely relaxed."

I **relax** my left foot, my left foot is completely relaxed.

I **relax** my left calf. My left calf is completely relaxed.

I **relax** my left thigh, my left thigh is completely relaxed.

I **relax** my hips and my pelvis. My hips and my pelvis are completely relaxed.

I **relax** my abdomen. My abdomen is completely relaxed.

I **relax** my back. My back is completely relaxed.

I **relax** the back of my neck and my shoulders. The back of my neck and my shoulders are completely relaxed.

I **relax** my right arm and my right hand. My right arm and my right hand are completely relaxed.

I **relax** my left arm and my left hand. My left arm and my left hand are completely relaxed.

I **relax** my face. My lower jaw, my lips, my tongue, my nose, my cheeks, my ears, my eyes, my eyebrows, my forehead and my scalp. My whole face is completely relaxed."

Then enjoy the feeling of calmness within you.

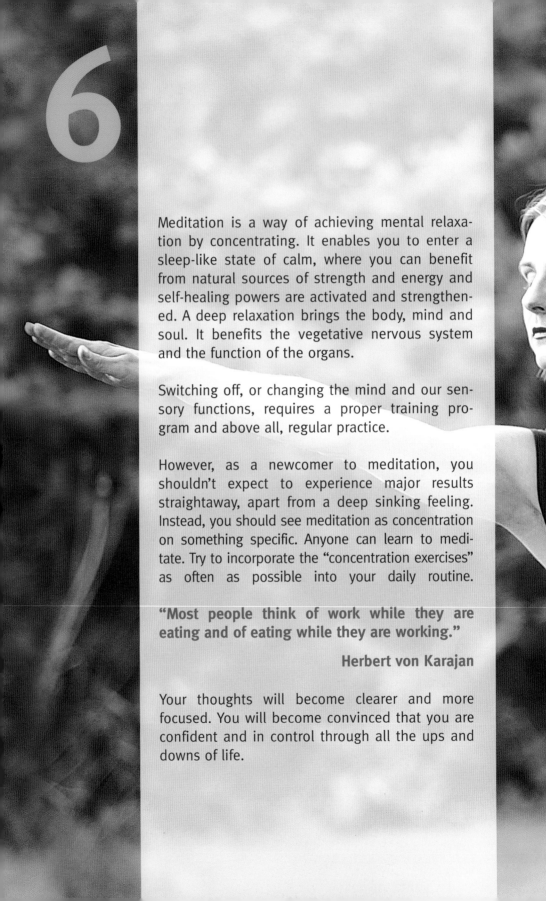

6

Meditation is a way of achieving mental relaxation by concentrating. It enables you to enter a sleep-like state of calm, where you can benefit from natural sources of strength and energy and self-healing powers are activated and strengthened. A deep relaxation brings the body, mind and soul. It benefits the vegetative nervous system and the function of the organs.

Switching off, or changing the mind and our sensory functions, requires a proper training program and above all, regular practice.

However, as a newcomer to meditation, you shouldn't expect to experience major results straightaway, apart from a deep sinking feeling. Instead, you should see meditation as concentration on something specific. Anyone can learn to meditate. Try to incorporate the "concentration exercises" as often as possible into your daily routine.

"Most people think of work while they are eating and of eating while they are working."

Herbert von Karajan

Your thoughts will become clearer and more focused. You will become convinced that you are confident and in control through all the ups and downs of life.

Meditation

Concentration

Concentrating, perceiving, centering and meditating all mean being centered in the here and now and becoming consciously involved in the present moment.

Children usually still have this undivided attention for what they are doing, but adults have to relearn it.

Types of Meditation

There are two kinds of meditation, abstract and objective meditation. As it is difficult for beginners to think of nothing, they should start with introductory exercises and concentrate on something concrete. This can be one's own breathing, or mantras like "Om," for example, or images or visual symbols.

Poses

A stable and comfortable position is important, but you must not go to sleep, for that is not the point of meditation. The most suitable pose is sitting cross-legged, or the Meditation position, in which the feet are placed in front of each other. By holding your thumb and index finger so that they are touching, you close the energy circuit. In yoga, this hand position is called mudra.

Tip:

Sit on a small, firm cushion or meditation cushion or a rolled up blanket. This makes your knees lower than your pelvis, and your pelvis tip forward slightly. Be careful not to hollow your back.

YOU CAN DO IT

The palms of your hands can either face upward or downward. If you sit completely upright, it is easier to turn your hands up. If the tension in your shoulders is still too great, start with the palms of your hands turned downward.

46

Breathing Meditation

This takes 5 or 10 minutes. Mentally go from your head to your toes, being aware of and relaxing each part of your body.

Monitor your breathing.

If you notice that deep concentration is making you hold your breath, sigh several times to relax all the muscles in your face, the back of your neck, your hands and your abdominal muscles.

How frequently are you breathing?

How deeply are you breathing?

Which lasts longer, your inhalation or your exhalation?

Then be aware of the space inside your trunk. Where can you feel movement in your body?

Can you feel your muscles contracting, moving or stretching?

Does your breathing make them relax?

Perhaps you can feel your chest rising and falling.

Can you feel muscle movements here? Or breathing movements?

Perhaps you can also feel these movements in your lower back? Or in your pelvis?

Where the breathing movements most?

Choose the area in which you can really feel the movements, and focus all your thoughts on this area.

Feel each individual breathing movement and the characteristics of each breath. Maybe some breaths are shorter than others. Do not influence them, just be aware of them. Your respiratory center, which controls your breathing, will automatically do everything right. The more deeply you relax, the calmer and more even your breathing will be.

Whenever a thought comes into your mind, let it go like water in a river.

Return patiently and single-mindedly to focusing on your breathing.

You can say the words "inhale" and "exhale" to yourself, to make it more difficult for other thoughts to enter your mind.

47

Fixing One's Gaze - Tratak

Look at an object, such as a candle flame, and concentrate all your thoughts on it. Do not let any other thoughts distract you. Look for as long as you can without blinking and without moving your eyes until your eyes water. Tears purify your eyes, but they shouldn't burn or hurt. Then close your eyes for a moment and visualize the flame in your mind's eye.

Repeat this process 2-3 times.

Tip:

If you cannot sit on the floor, sit on a chair. Do not relax into the chair; sit upright using your own strength.

Expansion Meditation

48

Sit up straight in a comfortable posture. Be aware of all the parts of your body that are touching the floor, so that you feel stable and firmly anchored to the floor. Inhale into these parts of the body and as you do so, imagine that you are stretching downward. You may experience a feeling of heaviness, or even lightness.

Then be aware of all the parts of your body that are facing the left. Your temple, ear, cheek, neck, shoulder, arm, hand, trunk, pelvis, leg and knee. Feel all these parts of your body and inhale into them. Notice how those parts of your body stretch each time you exhale. There is no limit to how much you can stretch.

Then immediately do the same thing on the right side of your body and stretch in all directions each time you exhale.

7 Programs for Beginners

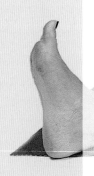

Positive Effects

The regular practice of yoga can get rid of back and neck pain, headaches and digestive problems, help relieve swollen legs and strengthen the immune system. You will be able to concentrate better and with time you will be much more aware of your body and feel more self-confident. Your muscles will also be more flexible and stronger, which is very useful in your daily life and in the prevention of injury.

B Training Programs

Training Guidelines

Exercise for at least 90 minutes once a week and incorporate a few breathing and relaxation exercises into your daily routine. You will, of course, make much greater progress if you practice every day.

If you can't manage to do 90 minutes in one go, divide your plan into morning breathing exercises, followed by the Sun Salutation and one or two back bends (see the chapter Special Training Programs).

Practice a few twisting postures during the day, especially if you have to sit down for long periods of time.

In the evening, place particular importance on the regenerating inverted poses, relaxing forward bends and a long final relaxation.

Beginners should hold the asanas for around 5 relaxed breaths and 2 minutes. The breaks between postures should last the same time as the asana itself.
At intermediate level, the postures can now be held for up to 3 minutes and the resting time can be reduced to half of the asana time.

Advanced yogis are able to relax so well during the asanas that they do not need resting time at all and the initial relaxation at the start can also be reduced to a minimum.

The final relaxation should always be included and should always last at least 10 minutes, or 20 minutes for beginners.

YOU CAN DO IT

Personal Prerequisites

Listen to your body as you perform the asanas and read the instructions thoroughly. If you are not yet able to carry out the asana as described, first do the simplified version. Give yourself time. Adapt the exercises to your physical condition. For example, if during the Seated Forward Bend you can only touch your head on your knees by rounding your back, your back will start to hurt and you may even suffer vertebral problems soon afterwards. You should only bend forward from the hips as long as you can keep your back in the physiologically correct position.

It would be wrong to round your back here. You will still feel the stretch in your hamstrings and therefore benefit from this exercise, as long as you relax each time you exhale. You may sometimes have to use objects like a cushion, stool or chair. In the long term, you will only enjoy and benefit from yoga if you perform the asanas at a level that corresponds to your individual ability.

The exercises themselves are obviously not detrimental to your health; on the contrary, they are beneficial.

If you already have damaged joints or injuries and symptoms of wear and tear in your active or passive musculoskeletal system, you may need to modify the yoga exercises. If this is the case, listen very carefully to your body and, ideally, ask an experienced yoga instructor for advice.

Environment

Exercise in a place where you feel good. It should be clean and tidy, but without necessitating a complete spring cleaning. Make sure that you will not be disturbed for the whole yoga session.

Wear warm, comfortable clothing. A non-slip yoga mat will make the standing poses easier. A warm blanket can intensify the relaxation effects. A meditation cushion will make sure you are sitting comfortably and can, make some exercises easier.

Make sure that you feel good about the whole situation.

YOU CAN DO IT

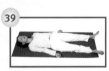
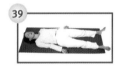

YOU CAN DO IT

3rd Session

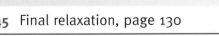

4th Session

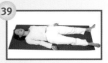

YOU CAN DO IT

5th Session

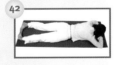

6th Session

YOU CAN DO IT

7th Session

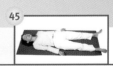

8th Session

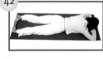

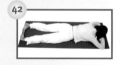

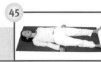

YOU CAN DO IT

9th Session

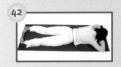

8
Special Training Programs

The following training programs consist of 5 different yoga sessions designed for specific purposes:

1.

Morning program – for an energizing start into the day

This program contains activating breathing and strength exercises. The relaxation element is deliberately reduced.

2.

Evening program – relaxation and regeneration

The aim is to reenergize the body and recover from the stresses of the day.

3.

Back program – for a strong back

Stress-relieving exercises let strained back muscles relax, so that they are ready to deal with the stresses of the day to come.

4.

Short program to do at home

For when you have little time to spare, but still want to keep up your yoga.

5.

Short program for the office

If you need a break from sitting at your desk and want to clear your head, this program is right for you.

YOU CAN DO IT

Morning Program – for an energizing start to the day

Do the breathing exercises standing up, and preferably in the fresh air.

1 Lung Activation, page 25

2 Gorilla, page 26

7 Mountain Pose, page 49

36 Focused Breathing standing up, page 118

3 Fire Reverence, page 27

9 Chest Opening, page 50

11 Self-Massage, page 52

10 Energy Exercise, page 51

19 The Wave, page 63

5 Sun Salutation, pages 32-3

23 Fish, page 77

25 Inclined Plane, page 83

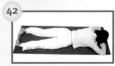

42 Reversed Corpse Pose, page 125

26 Cobra, page 86

41 Pose of a Child, page 124

30 Spinal Twist, easy variation, page 99

33 Tree, page 106

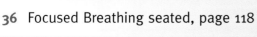

36 Focused Breathing seated, page 118

Evening program – relaxation and regeneration

YOU CAN DO IT

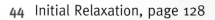

YOU CAN DO IT

5.

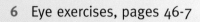

Index

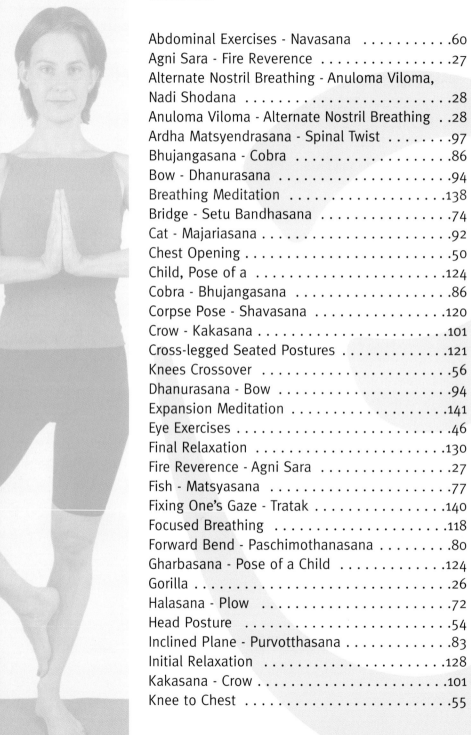

Photo Credits

Cover Photo: DPA Picture-Alliance, Germany
Back Cover: Rudolf A. Hillebrecht
Inside Photos: Rudolf A. Hillebrecht
Cover Design: Jens Vogelsang, Germany

You can contact the author at:
m.schwichtenberg@web.de